NICE NOSE

Buck Downs

WASHINGTON, D.C. : : 2023

In addition to appearing as a series of
stickers and other author-published
ephemera, the poems in *NICE NOSE*
appear, sometimes in earlier versions,
on the Instagram account
@thesomethingfornothing.

1813 Burke St., S.E.
Washington, DC 20003

www. buckdowns .com

Manufactured in the United States of America

I.

Have It Your Way

I learned to stop
        laying down
the ultimatum
        from people
who shrugged and said,
        okay, man —
have it your way
        as they left

a higher calling
than making a living,
        that's my job —

    sweet invisible
    means of support

love won't shut up —

no you shut up —

when you work for yourself
it's like everyone's your boss
                    — for Tom Waits

if you think god's job is difficult
            consider the person
who does god's performance review

      consider the secretary
who handles the scheduling

my favorite place to smoke
is in my own house

and I secretly adore
that it smells like
a sweaty ashtray

even after I've been
gone for two weeks

WHERE AM I

people! stop

asking me

where you are

money transfer

he got a pay cut

hell he got
'em all cut

bad apartment

    tough lover

    that bedroom

    had some teeth

SON OF A BITCH

what can you say
when someone hateful
loves you

SLOW COMB

 — for Elaine

I don't think
about your body

except you keep
bringing it up

cyclone song

    I wound up spinning
    I wound up wound up

       that's how it is
       when you wind up
         with a cyclone

PORT OF MORROW
                    — for John B.,
                        in Boardman, Ore.

    cold storage
    no toilets

the cost of a toilet
is small potatoes

they are just jerks

[time lapse]

    sleep is too important
to spend in idle dreaming

    dreams have more to do
than be your raw material

PEANUT BUTTER

peanut butter and
           jackfruit
        sandwich

I had a nap
for dinner

FIVE SECOND RULE

all the dirt in my house
is created by me
or by the creatures
who feed on me

so I feel safe
eating any food
that hits the floor

THE ANGEL OF MERCY

wore a festive mask
she made for herself
from a vacation shirt
    she used to wear
        back when
she went on vacations

          — for @carolinabeachhfuller

FAMOUS LAST WORDS

come on
what have
you got
to lose

a fidget button
for pushing

some unlabeled
trap-door
I always
fall for

my desire to push
the button,

I have no idea —
and what does this do —

SCREAMING DOG IN THE BACKGROUND

and when people ask
    why does your dog
        scream like that
            I say
she's very advanced

caking in a big way

going on a cake date

letting the cake drive you home

REMEMBER

an algorithm

is always a guess

never an answer

nonstopping

I've been
missing you
since I met you

LEAF BLOWER

you'd be surprised
          how fragile
cops are these days

now that everything
has been weaponized

god is not afraid
    of the darkness —

    "it's where I do
        my best work."

& there I was —
so distracted
by world events
I lost the lid
to the peanut butter

TRUST ME

every guy my age
starts to look a little
like an off duty cop

PROVERB

a guy who learns
to laugh at himself
will never lack
for entertainment

RESOLUTION

stop responding
    to people
    you don't know
and who aren't
addressing you
    anyway

[crème brumaire]

    I get lost
in it, watching
my girl burn through
a pepperoni-
pizza like mist

scraping the place,
    I mean plate —
scraping it clean,
       I mean
scraping it clean —

[gasoline]

everybody knows
        when you say
a dollar sixty-eight
            you mean
a dollar sixty-nine

[joe namath]

    everything
about joe namath
has grown smaller
with age — except
    his giant
        white teeth

I Don't Know

         is one of the most
     useful stock phrases
ever — I don't know why
         more people don't
     use it more often

WHY I DON'T HAVE A COUCH

I would
lay on it
all day

I wish I had
my little map —
the one I made,
    but I don't —

I couldn't pick up
where I left off —
I had to pick up
    somewhere else

II.

THE HAZARDS

when you have to
head for the hazards
as a kind of compromise —

"I'll get into
this trouble,
then I'll get out —
here's how!"

auto-correct
    is a kind
    of slurred speech

    we are all
speaking too fast

some of the busiest
    people I know
        will tell you
        they are good
at doing nothing

what has this moment
      made obsolete — Joe Hall

you just have to forget
that you are being watched
as often as you can

and notice how much time
you spend looking at yourself

ON RECORDING

one thing
about my voice
is I shouldn't
listen to it

THREE BREAKFASTS A DAY

bagel w/fried egg & cheese

egg sandwich w/cheese and bacon

scrambled eggs & hash browns
                    w/bacon

my mom was like,

    you can't google
        worth a fuck,
            gimme that —

magic is accidental —
anyone tells you
         they *know how*
    to *do magic* —
they're just putting you on —

[nostalgia]

you can't miss
what you don't
remember

c'mon,

all this capital
isn't going
to just spend itself

the invisible forms
       of credit, no
    credit whatever —

this is how poetry is like

    if you have to ask
    you can't afford it

              — for @jordandavispoet

THE SMALL PILLOW

I sleep with
a small pillow

primitive form
of a stuffed animal

for something
to do with my hands
in my sleep

[nobody hates television]

we love it —
    that's why
we must kill it

if you don't get that,
    you haven't been
        watching

[my regimen]

I keep it
        sweet
with chemicals

[poem for twitters]

if it feels like
you are reading
an argument
    two robots
    are having
with each other
you may be right

and just what does a clock
know about time

up late is better
    than up early

even if the clocks
    say it's the same

caper flick

— after @matthewklone

they had to take
      one more
   vacation
before they retired

yeah
your love
is a rose
I get it

— for @jimbehrle

I don't buy
    tough love
    outside
the bedroom

the princess & the pea

some little
stone in bed
that gave off
a great
vibration

crushed cadaver botanica

I think I never told you
but I suck at the santeria

THE EMAIL

if I had read
the message twice
before writing
back once I might
not have needed
to write at all

[for Mayakovsky]

many are the poets
     who claim to have had
a true conversation
     with the sun — the sun
          has disavowed
               any knowledge
          of their actions —

     anyone who has looked
directly into the sun
     can tell you the truth
is not the whole story —

three things || two hands

I always need
my mouth. the mouth
    comes in handy

on a blue t.v.

left to my own
        devices
I would still be
        on my knees

                              the foist of time
                              it puts on you

it's getting late sooner
around here these days

I'll be getting up
before I go to bed

— after N.J. Paik

I don't know
just as much
as the next guy —

and the next guy
don't know plenty —

[on working together]

     two good men,
     friends of mine —
both with a little edge
to them — no surprises
     there — will they cut
        each other up — or
keep each other sharp

in support of nothing

what you do in front
          of everyone

the less said about it
the better, with nothing
     being best of all

[queen size]

      I slept
   all over
        that bed

[gravy]

gravy on the breakfast,
hitting breakfast hard —

let there be gravy
    on everything,
    let my friends all
have the gravy they want

        — for @smushdub

it is often hard to know
how tired I am
at any given moment
and what effect
that may have
on the decisions
I am about to make

[for @sam_roeck]

we don't remember the past
we can't predict the future
        & the present
    doesn't even exist

        everybody thinks
            they're the expert,
                then they find out

[love poem]

the moon is made
     out of love
         that's why
     it's so hard,
etc.

one of those stitch in time
        save nine things, except
in reverse and because
I did not take the time
        now I do the nine

if you don't stop
telling yourself
that's a perfectly
good piece of paper
you'll end up buried
alive in that stuff

like hospital santa

you never see
    the same kid
a second time

variation on a theme
by @zaher.maged

I look at cigarettes
their butt
isn't your butt

[some girls]

when the whip comes down

it was just my imagination
    (running away with me)

like some jubilee
year when all our
    achievements
    are forgiven
and we can really
    start fresh with
    nothing to lose

an ice cream cone
     that could lick
        itself
would find it has
       lost its
reason for being

[sunday afternoon]

if it can't be cleaned
it must not be dirty

we do not answer the phone
because it is not for us

paleo economics

red meat is like
money you can eat —
tasty money —

funny how digging
a hole feels like
climbing
when your head
is up your ass

talking trash about people
                is a kind of
talking trash about yourself

        if you want to put
                somebody down
you have to go down there
                with them

the bat has its own
art of clicks
and cries

we could call it a song
if not for our fears

sometimes we don't want
to hit the bull's eye — there
    are so many good places
        you can land your shot
without even trying — a tight
    cluster around the heart —

I was working
for a candy-
          store and they
let me get sick

I wasn't the first

this will fix itself

III.

they say we are all one
but I think it must be
        more like three quarters
because so many of us
are not entirely here

cat on a toaster

something smells good
and warm and weird
I'm out of here

2 between & 3 ahead

sometimes the language
      problem presents
          itself as
a matter of counting

          what you
      are thinking of
as a math problem
      to be solved

   turns out to be
a gift certificate
      to be shared

[the optimist]

I'm banking
on gravity

to hold me down —
so far, so good —

the way I feel

tonight I could be

in the emergency

room tomorrow

sometimes I look
at my appliance

and I say, shoot,
I don't even know
why I'm turning you on

my sweet little phone chirps
and I always think it's you
    but it's just my phone,
    battery low again —

did my house
catch fire
& I not
even know

if your house
catches fire

save the fire
save the fire

[experimental poem]

    say *I could use
a cup of coffee*
    in the poem — see
    if anybody
        gets me one —

taking out
the garbage
feels like such
a win
I want to go
out and bring it
back in

[the fog of memory]

when I saw it for the first time
I thought I knew what it was

    by the time I saw it
           a third time,
I was no longer sure

[poem for influencers]

if you can't set
a good example

you may get to be
an object lesson

[trick knee]

I have developed
    a trick knee

I do not much
    like this trick

if what you have
is a police problem
police will come
& solve you

[the algorithm]

a word of mouth
        that works
    without you

whether or not
you have something
you want to say

I crash
     test
tele-
     phones

[for @wassupgina]

I'm sure Stevie must have said,
        "Fucking Christine! Gets away!
            with MURDER!"

        a time or two — I mean,
we've all had a friend like that —

the lovelies who blithely glide
over the brambles in which
        we tangle — the bullshit
            of men and life,
the trickery of attention
and currency and desire —

                they glide, and they rise,
                    and then they go,
                and then they are gone —

[television poem]

every family
is a crime family

if you don't have
some ill-gotten
gains to covet
why are you even
having children

money makes
nothing happen
and yet — men die
every day
for what it is
they find there —

the most rock'n'roll
place I've ever been

was my own
bedroom folks
true story

[the wayfarer]

sunglasses that shade
our eyes from the sun,

protecting us from
    the very thing
we came here to see

[battle refund]

your battles can be
        fully refunded
whenever you want
    to fight them again

[small talk]

she's all like, treat you
        like an animal,

        I'm like, animals
treat me pretty good

it's a thin line,
      America —

you want to get fired
      but you don't want
to get arrested —

when you're the only one
adding comments to your
        post   maybe it's time
to take the whole thing down

[television poem]

scooby-doo
    doesn't

even know
    he's dead —

that's not true!

scooby-doo
    is back!

and looking
    better

than ever!

the red toyota (Taylor's version)

                    never mind
                the red toyota!

                then it's red toyota
                    after red toyota
        in the rain this afternoon

[THE NAME OF YOUR LIFE]

when I woke up there was
a television
in my mouth —

it was showing
the name of my life —
the secret name —

everyone watched
what I could not see,
they heard
what I did not know —

Made in the USA
Middletown, DE
15 August 2023